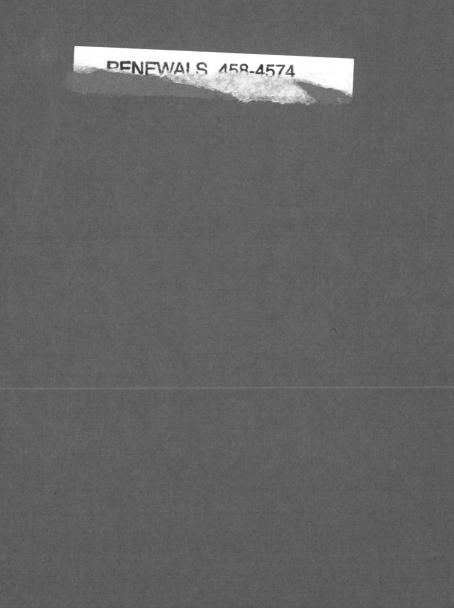

A FIRE BY THE TRACKS

A FIRE BY
THE TRACKS

poems by
Patrick Todd

OHIO STATE UNIVERSITY PRESS
Columbus, Ohio

Library of Congress Cataloging in Publication Data

Todd, Patrick
  A fire by the tracks.

  I. Title.
PS3570.0393FS   1982   811'.54   82-14411
ISBN 0-8142-0343-4

In memory of my father, brother and twin sons.
This book is for my wife and three children.
For more family and friends,
too many to name.
With special thanks to
Richard Hugo and A.R. "Archie" Ammons.

Acknowledgements

"Country Wedding" was previously published in *Choice*, No. 10 (1977), *Montana Gothic*, No. 5 (Winter, 1977), and *Where We Are: The Montana Poets* (Missoula, Montana: CutBank/Smoke-Root Press, 1978). "Dinner at the Mission" appeared in *The Paper SAC* (now *The Clark Fork Free Press*), Vol. III, No. 5 (May, 1980). "Francis of Assisi" was also included, as "St. Francis," in *Where We Are: The Montana Poets*, as was "Furnace Tenders," first published by the Pulp Press Book Publishers. "Michael Gripping Satan's Hair" was previously published in the *Ohio Journal*, Vol. III, No. 2; "Pigeons in the Ghost Tower," in *Borrowed Times*, Vol. III, No. 14 (April 1–15, 1975); and "Poem for Far-off Cries in the Portland Zoo" in *Sojourners*, Vol. VIII, No. 11 (November, 1979), and *The Stream Invents a Smile*, an anthology published in 1980 by the Poets and Writers in Schools Program of the Montana Arts Council. "Roast Dog" also first appeared in *The Paper SAC*, Vol. III, No. 5; and "Sheep and Pigs at Pablo" (as "Sheeps and Pigs") in *GiltEdge, New Series*, Vol. I (1980). "Slaughterhouse" was first published in *Choice*, No. 10 (1977); "South End Wrecking" (as "Warm Wind") in *CutBank*, No. 1 (Autumn, 1973) and the *Ohio Journal*, Vol. III, No. 2. Several of these same poems and others in the present volume also appeared in Mr. Todd's previously published collection *Fire in the Bushes* and his chapbook *The Iron Walrus*, published in 1977 and 1979, respectively, by Clearwater. The approval of editors and publishers of their inclusion herein is gratefully acknowledged.

CONTENTS

I

II

III

I.

NIGHT FIRE IN BROOKLYN

April '42 storm troopers crash
through Berlin cedar groves
roar up to a farmhouse and dump the child's coffin
looking for a dead title or something
Tears roll down the old grandfather's face and his hair
stands above his ears like little wings
By '52 in New York four hundred thousand people
have swarmed from ship holds usually reserved for sheep and hogs
They come for freedom to learn the exact value
of a few hidden coins and dead

weight of steel girders
stacked to buy bread and a thirty-cent
broom   Outside the factory smoke
welders' beads tie the girders together and the girders
go up forever   Here immigrants learn the exact
twenty dollars too much for a rickety

flat with Little Orphan Annie's
zero eyes on a dimestore cup
Tonight snow falls silent on Brooklyn and Queens
It swirls and hangs over vacant lots a mysterious white fleece
New ice   Thunder of trains underground
For a split second an old man looms dark and ominous
warming his hands over flames inside
a brown steel drum

WAKING IN A TRAIN YARD

Morning sun and the mint-green maples
Frost on the grass and it's May 5th
Frost on the train engines and ice gleams
along eaves of the roundhouse
What's it like mornings to wake cold in a boxcar?
To roll over   Slide down   To find frost on the sway
bar and couplings   Last night another tramp walked
the yard till his feet swelled inside his boots
and he laid down in wet grass wishing he
could crawl inside the ground
Wearing a big army field coat he sits down
in a cafe this morning and orders coffee
Imagine the first cup poured in a white building
before Christ   probably in Venezuela
Coffee beans the color of brown skin
They are the brown of Moroccan dowry beads
Trappist rosaries   Of genuine mahogany barstools
The licorice black espresso beans are heaped in bags
on coffee wagons like a cache of raw money
Still coffee is the one thing that allows a break
from the cold for a dime and five nickels

*

Hair   snarled radish leaves   Eyes
dead to the world   Finally in a warm place
the man sits with both hands around walls
of a porcelain cup   Imagine asking
him questions concerning Poland or the pope

4

A month back the president was shot
Imagine asking the man about violence and divorce
Once in a window in San Francisco   I saw grapes heaped
with apples and bananas   With big purple eggplant
oranges   pineapples   and avocados sprayed
wet next to smoked salmon   Smoked beef
Roast duck   Huge cakes of cheddar and provolone
Salami hung overhead with long coiled tubes
of Hungarian sausage   And nudging thick walls of a tank
six lobsters waited to be split open like giant
pistachio nuts   Outside the delicatessen
rich smell of coffee filled the street

*

To a man who sleeps on the ground   in cars
under warehouse docks and in all-night
laundromat chairs   chatter in cafes sounds
like chickens   It sounds like someone rattling
tinfoil   or the jumbled rantings of displayed televisions
In his whole life the man in the cafe has never uttered
a word concerning the mayor or Queen Elizabeth
He lifts his cup and the steam alone
is worth the first dime paid   Coffee   Coffee without
eggs   Without buttered toast   Or a slice of ham
shaped like North Dakota   There are endless
stories about soldiers marching to their death
Endless stories about their women who waited
This poem is about bandages unraveled   Raw sores dry now
Blue and yellow harbor pillars rise in fog above the lost boat
This morning the man bummed thirty-five cents hardly asking

And if he thought about it   this moment suspended
in time   is worth more than three long
nights in bed with sheets   More than coat and
boots of sheepskin   For this moment off the street
with coffee he'd pay the last gold
coin raised from the bottom of the sea

FURNACE TENDERS

Morning in the brick change house
forty men pull on dries
Squeak and slam of lockers   First whistle
Then the long slow trek across the yard
Two boys file on the elevator with the men
Fourteen furnaces big as houses and four stories up
Have to knock the floors out of furnace number five
Only three foot ceilings inside
so we break and shovel on our backs
Fierce burning of the eyes   Sweat and cough
Two-hour stretches we shovel dry chunks of zinc out porthole
    doors
Graveyard operators hit the feed floor first thing
Dump in sacks of arsenic   Run down to the next floor
Long iron bar breaks up zinc inside
the orange blast   Plastic face mask
Leather gloves up to the elbows with canvas
apron to ward off the heat
Ten minutes facing that fire

and you run outside for three
Ten more and back out
Chunks broken down   Foreman in the shack
Sweep up zinc dust that floats like water
on the steel floor   Take five
Once a boy caught his broom in the conveyor
The foreman found him   arm   shoulder and head crushed
to pulp   Hook up your coat anywhere in the zinc leach
The next morning it hangs in shreds

Thirty years in the roasters
and dry rasping breaks in the lungs
Some get milk leg   The skin
bags paste white and men sit out half their shifts
on the benches   One guy   ten kids   endless payments
and pictures of Christ all over his house
pushes the bar into the face
of a routine orange blast and forgets
Forgets he grabbed the guard loop and his hand's exposed
Caught between the bar and a steel beam the bones
mash like a bag of peanuts
Morley dies and the guy without a hand
gets his soft job

COUNTRY WEDDING

All nervous in country lace the bride
rode down the mountain with her father
wagon reins springing easy in the early sun
Fifty mums banked the church walls white
Thick cream candles   The groom sat
mute for the stiff picture
Both hands closed big as hammers

Women owned this time around the holy cake
The old fathers   faces puffed red
from years of whiskey and the blazing wheat
waited out weddings like a funeral
Even the sleepy minister hated
circles of screaming kids and spotted
a yellow toy he'd love to crush

Gone the bride in white lace
whose wedding moon lit up a long lazy string
of geese over McGuinnigan's Pond
Now the farmers' sons grow mean in town
a boy beat a hole in a boxcar
with a hundred-pound furnace iron
Gone twenty horses steaming in the barn

POEM FOR GORDON A. PRICHARD AND FAMILY

Hunting parts in the wilderness
of junk on his brother's acre
Or the whole family clomping downstairs
past someone's three year old wailing
at the walls in a Pittsburgh tenement
Finally pulling into Des Moines at two A.M.
And pulling out of Butte at dawn
Here they are at the door   Gordon A. Prichard and family
Four dollars and twenty-three cents   a quart of milk
some Cheetoes and gas tank empty after burning
their tires bald on the smoldering
highways to reach Missoula   And what can
Gordon do to feed his wife and kids?
He can tear an engine apart and put it back together
clean as a clock   He can swamp out bars till the sun comes up
Or nail studs in a row till his hand freezes
numb to the hammer   He can work twelve hours and rack
out on the gas station floor
Or slump in the cab of a truck ready to go
again in an hour   And what can we
do for him? A hot meal for his family
One bag of groceries and fresh tank of gas will be plenty
His second son will live the same way when he grows up
The first will join the Army early and drink
his life into a grumbling stupor
His oldest daughter will succeed running
a beauty parlor   His other girl will

disappear without record while the last boy lives
in and out of a house truck in Casper
O roaders of the world   gigolos   robbers   pickers
and part-time welders   O healer of the mare's split hoof
It's grease for the axle turned the first
wheels holy   Lust for the road scattered Lot's
family homeless   And not a flick
of mercy for the peasants buried under
Rome   Toledo   and Uganda

BLACK CHRISTMAS

It's a dark Christ hangs
on a bunker wall
Wind roars down giant blizzard wheels
and whole companies huddle in dead mens' blankets
When the storm lifts at Gumrak the moon grows
huge and terrible to a man hiding in the belly of a dead
mule   Two soldiers ride up
Long boots squeak icy saddles and rifles

riddle the mule like a hay bale
The black lily of a gramophone wails hymns
in a warehouse hospital
Three villages grow forests

of wood crosses and each
tractor and cannon in a drift monuments
this miserable Christmas
January comes and von Paulus won't budge
to enemy offers   Russian tanks roll ''geese on water''
and Hitler's Sixth
Army is butchered in the snow

FORTY LINES FOR UMBERTO ROCA

At ten below the moon freezes
thin above the east
mountains   Not one sound in the pine
till the midnight train steams and thunders in
giant wheels squealing nightmare tons of steel and ice
Halfway down the string a little
Mexican slides off a boxcar
and soon as he hits the snow he feels
he can't feel a thing from the knees down
Bone cold   Ravaged with fever under a warehouse dock
One week in the hospital and his feet crack
and bake black as old woman's shoes
What hell matches the wrong
freight north and a thousand miles from
everything but a row

of blue pills?   In back
of the poorhouse center I open his
gunny sack for whatever
we can wash   One world war overcoat   blanket
balled socks and wool shirt snarled around stone hard
bread and crumbled cheese   Only this hairnet
filled with ladies' elegant

evening gloves seems strange
And the twenty-odd dimestore rings
he asks me to save
Umberto Roca   tough little hundred-pound

Mexican with wild bramblebush hair and Fu Manchu whiskers
where are you now that doctors sent you south on a jet
with new swivel feet? Are you palming coins
on a side street in Fresno?
Or did some sweet lady take you home
as the stumped and roving mascot for her
crazy dogs and kids?

NEOLA

Kept a small wild park   thick with pine
and cottonwoods   a hundred sparrows wheeled
into rain woods after a storm
When spring run-off dropped away from
banks of The Clarkfork   Clayton Horne and his
buddies claimed half a mile of the shore line
Those were the years they pulled in browns and whitefish
from the bridge   And waded waste deep through soaking weeds
to see winos lying around a campfire   Or the godawful
sight of Rex Chamley stripping down for a swim
in his greasy longjohns   One night
a huge wild moon swelled over the river
and trees   Only his second summer at the mill
and still no more than a sheepish boy
Clayton stood on the porch of an old clapboard house
above the train yard while two friends waited behind the hedge
in a pickup   A small black woman opened the door
and after brief talk in velvet chairs she led him to
a room   complete with antique tassle
lamp shades   burgundy silk sheets and a mirror
on the ceiling   Clayton Horne has never
been to Paris or finished the book
about a dark lady of Madrid   Still Neola
was plenty for any boy from a country town or the city
This morning   twenty years later   he is simply
a man waiting for her to cross the icy street in front of his car
One hand lugging a big suitcase   The other waving stupid
traffic out of her way   She is catching

the 9:03 this time   The train already rumbling
and steaming behind the station
Dark lady with a side-long glint in her eye
and rough laugh   Once he leaned down to
kiss the yellow butterfly on her lovely round hip
and learned the total price for the full dinner of his pleasures
Who is he to her now? Banker in a little car on business?
Family man? No one she remembers in the lost faces
of a hundred men   When she waves him off
dull in his dapper hat and gloves   there is
a reason   Clayton Horne hasn't even been to New York
But he has been to Neola's at the dead end of 4th Street
And grows more careful each day with
what he gives and takes in the fast world

FRANCIS OF ASSISI

At dusk mile-long clouds
stream orange
above the sun going down
Purple drifts over the mountains far as the sea
After all is said and done   all passion
for wife and lovers gone
No one   Not even a room this time
Only this walk along the road   yellow trees   sky
the bright cold grass   Tonight under giant ponderosa
slow blue flames rise from blackberries
and the whole bush flares up

blazing white   On the climb
like this to La Verna
a hundred birds swarmed St. Francis
The next morning Leo peeked around the secret hut
to see his brother soar high as the trees

High in the Sistine Chapel
fury of brushes
lifted God and creation on the ceiling
In the basement Michelangelo chiseled ripples of silk
in marble   There's no holy word for the need
to be alone   In the far woods
only this steady light gleams in oil
of the burro's eye

II.

PIGEONS IN THE GHOST TOWER

No priest founded this small town
Money from the east raised
hotel and depot along the sleepy Clarkfork
paneled the bank mahogany and burned
grapes around the copper cages
What could be more innocent than Worden and Higgins
posed with store goods laid out for the stiff picture?
Missoula means "chilly waters of surprise" and more than once
a fire-haired whore chased some logger off
her porch with a butcher knife
In 1892 four stage robbers hung like socks
from a cottonwood so the timid priest settled three
blocks back from the town

center and painted his steeple
soft gold   Now the mills
lay off half their men   pigeons dot
the ghost depot tower forlorn as the parked engines
On the tower only one pigeon now
Wait   another one lands on the east face

upper right hand window
Three more drop to nothing in the rocks
A strange new guy in town walks
into The Mercantile holding his bedroll close
in both arms   He might as well lie down in the shirts
piled stark white and useless
as the icy sheets   This winter nothing
short of another war will open up
the mills full swing

ST. MARTIN'S

Tonight a full round moon
Windows glow orange
as isinglass and leaves underfoot crunch
air light against the far-off roar of traffic
Autumn nights a raw animal greed
wells up in some to escape winter for salty beaches
This far north a gray Ford from Alabama stops at St. Martin's
The old man   a walrus in filthy coveralls
slumps in an office chair
Hung strange over his head   baroque

icons of Mary and Christ
Twin desk pens gleam black as knitting
needles   The solid oak coat rack
too rich for a man comfortable with engines
With steel shavings piled

like flour   A few
dollars worth a handful of twigs
With his family bundled in the car
hungry and three thousand miles
from home   he could sleep easy on the plush carpet
And for the priest in a dapper silk robe
he can work
like a horse for meals

POVERELLO

About six   two-feet drifts
in the morning dark
Only a monk would love thick ice hanging
from the roof   Or love first morning
sounds   lobsters clicking
in the pipes   On the table   rags
stiff as peeled bark bring thoughts of August heat
What could I say to the lady raped by a trucker
and left to heal in this gray house
You can rest here   Stay as long as you want for once
Even the pockmarked sink looked good in her single room
Miles off two antelope look up startled in the picture
of blowing grass   There's little relief
in the dry board floor   But towel
Soap   Fresh sheets   The gold-speckled
boomerang ashtray lights up a dimestore shelf
in every town across the states

*

Racked by years of withdrawal
from wine mud sleep   one
old roader comes back a second morning now
shivering against the wall by the parking lot
He nods away in the warm sun
His green blanket   peed on through three children
stretched oblong by the dog and flapped thin on the way
to ten picnics was brought here washed

*

Even cream-light skin wrapped
in blue couldn't hide
your badger hair   Your birth opened
a hundred doors that close now with drum percussion
Murry Yellow Horse   A name too long above
the school racks   Your sisters' legs
brown and dry as drumsticks
Even your foster mother's eyes gleamed so black
they made the blonde world nervous
Today the poorest church in town and Welfare...Murry
get you out of jail for a long icy Greyhound ride
to Rapid City   Once a plains Indian town
now only a ring of friends wait
already drunk by noon   Cold wind   North
Tin of your trailer shines so thin it creaks in storms
So cold and clear on still nights your
radio crackles in the stars

BILLY

Bright as tree bulbs   red velvet
fantails zoom through rows
of bubbles   Through long green lettuce bushes
In and out of holes in the rock
Every Saturday Billy stands for hours
hands folded big as a ball   giant shoulders stooped
over colored tanks   And dead perfect the part
in his hair plastered wet by his auntie
Red fish zooming and zooming
Most people look away from Billy but fish
eyes stare straight out sideways   same as a chickens
or eyes of a bike chain   Slow as brooms his big shoes shuffle
to another tank   Moonfish drift up pale balloons
No…he likes red ones zooming and shuffles
back to the first tank   Fantails
quick as sparks and beautiful sky-blue rocks

on the bottom   This is the same
feeling he loves in church
When everyone sings the whole room fills up
with light   One time he saw kids hitting
A boy fell and blood under the monkey bars made Billy
run away to his auntie   Away from kids at the school hitting
In another tank   black lizard fish
creek along the rocks

with rubbery feet   And the moray
eel   alone in his hole
breathes in and out like a soft vacuum cleaner hose

Billy shuffles out the glass door
Past the hydrant yellow as a crayon
and snow heaped like brown
sugar on the corner   The boys kept hitting
One fell   Then the terrible screaming
All night orange tubes hummed in back of his static radio
Now he's learned to turn it on   most nights Billy
lies awake where no one knows
Eyes wide as a fish's he watches the tubes
glow inside the wooden box   And while he drifts
away the bright fish come back humming
inside the warm green water

CHRISTMAS EVE IN MEDFORD

Down from the Medford depot
neon over The Salvation Army hums
fire red in the dark
I shower and bunk near men twice my age
and barely choke down thick gruel served from a big
steel bowl   Can't say two words
where winos bald as angels line up for cake
and Christmas hymns crackle

over a blue radio   One A.M. I wake
to the whitest man in the world snoring under
his sheet   Then dress and hurry

through whirling snow
for the night express to San Francisco
Gold morning sun brings warm relief
on Noe Street   A little altar lit up with candles
Mexican lace and blood red poinsettias
a small miracle

MARCH AND THE BRIGHT CROCUS

This winter even the blowdown
on the boiler froze
Two months of ice-ragged elms and the river
jammed solid   Early-morning sun now my daughter hunts
feathers under the pine   I smolder first
spring laps around a soggy track
Is the little man Berton Laird   giant belly
filled with three hundred winter beers   a barometer
for my own shrinking bulge?

Let the crocus measure release
this spring   Last month a ninety-pound woman
raged against everyone while starving alone
in her single room   When I brought church-relief
groceries her bony cat devoured

the tuna with his back hunched
tight as wire   That same
week police found a man living alone on a hundred-
pound bag of cornmeal   Crocus blaze open
flames in the bright sun   White   purple   gold
Ah crocus!   The wonderful snow
of swan feathers

LEAVING A PLAINS MISSION

At noon a lone engine idles
under the water tower
The brakeman lays back with his head
propped against his lunch box
And farther out a hawk turns frozen on a post
where nothing else moves in the void of wheat
It's so hot here the tower shimmers
in the sun and you'd swear
any sparrow might hit the wires
in a shower of sparks
When night comes and the priest doesn't
return home the old woman across
the road circles the church
She circles his house with a flashlight
steps into his back porch and back out
to turn the sprinkler off
Up at dawn   Father Hennon walked
over to say mass for six women and one man
He walked back for two swallows from his flask of bourbon
Packed all his clothes and books into his car
and headed out toward Fargo
Every morning this winter he squeaked
over ice in the dark to say mass
Four times   head bare to the wind
he prayed for the dead to be buried under snow
and blowing weeds   And he could almost
hear the stories of his life hum through wires
laced between farm roofs

Tonight the old woman winds his
hose into a heap by the porch
She leans a shovel against the wall
Walks back across the road and opens the slow
blue flame under her coffee pot determined
to wait up all night
Ten thousand chicken heads
whacked off on the block
Train loads of cattle hauled to their
slaughter each fall   And pigs
sliced open clean as the lard in vats
How do men hold back disgust for an old woman
looking in the priest's windows?
When winter cakes the town with ice
four widows hobble to the church
in coats old as snow
Forty-three years two candles on the sandal
wood altar gleam perfect blades of light at dawn
All their prayers rising rich
with the blood of animals   the women know
certain as ever now the third new priest
sent over from Minot
will serve their God or go

MICHAEL GRIPPING SATAN'S HAIR

All old schools have the same smell
Food from the big kitchen
and wood floors lit with fresh wax
When I was a kid the desks were bolted to flat skis
Chalk dust stained the blackboards with endless blizzards
and our first-grade teacher swatted our butts
with a two-foot hose   Mornings she
folded down map-size pictures of Adam and Eve
Christ wept in the suffering garden and Joseph stood tall
and beautiful in this bright colored coat
Thieves from the bushes attacked and left him
in the sand   God and evil

planted deep in our small hearts
I remember   ball   coat
book   cup   and words about Dick and Jane
Mostly they played on grandfather's little white farm
New car   Brand new barn and the whole family
happy together with perfect hair

Our fathers drove old beaters
to the smelter   Abandoned
mothers drew monthly welfare and Bonnie
Deshner got knocked up in eighth grade
One Indian kid lived alone with an old old man
No wonder the giant pictures filled with pain
In the best one St. Michael leans down raising his sword
for the big swath   Satan's
hair locked firm in his other hand

SLAUGHTERHOUSE

Once a farm girl wore red to the dance
The next morning her grandmother
told how spiders gleam in the eyes of roosters

At the new domed slaughterhouse
giant fans roar millions of feathers up in smoke
Dock trays of liver heap like squid

The last truck pulls out
All through the night four thousand hens
thunder like snow in their cages

GOING HOME IN EKALAKA

Alone again in a little town
I open a door to the
school gym where a janitor works the north
bleachers   Radio going   Slow knock of broom
A cold wind jiggles the last blades
of light on the ceiling
Only a few years ago the grocery here
roared up like wheat while firemen fumbled with snarled hose
A woman sobbed by a car and the crowd stood helpless
as if watching executions four centuries back
Weekends a teacher hunts fossils
under shale drifts and only a few bones

are missing from the duck-billed
dinosaur in the basement
of the school   On my way home
to the yellow motel I watch a man lift from a tub
of acid   a radiator clean as a dry beehive

He studies it solid
understood and useful as a gun
or good plough   No wonder
St. Anthony's face shines soft as a child's
in the brick church   Whoever formed his dull gaze
forgot how each autumn the humble saint
watched hundreds of swallows swirl
and dive below a cliff   And the salmon runs
glitter flames in the sea

THREE TOWNS ON THE PLAINS

Six months old and she lies here
with her legs folded
Her eyes nod off a long terrible sleep
Six months   three boys break
this horse down with sticks and she already owns
one spot behind these funky motel cabins
No one will touch her again
She'll never toss her head or run
In Babb someone will come out and shoot'r
or she'll die in the brutal winter
Last year snow buried a road grader in two hours
Sounds funny to think of it left running and only the exhaust
hole found smoking from the bank
A man was killed this spring when someone
drove over and over him with a pickup

*

One car pulls in at Loma
where a grocer stares at nothing
from the door   His thick hands grip a cup
and thermos   Each night he locks the bar
he must hate the doorbell tinkle
Must hope some boy will hammer the screen
Not with questions for a room but news of violence
down the road or a burning farm
Just passing through most talk of love
for simple things   Crows work the slough toward evening

It would be fun to raise cows   People leave these
booths old and brown   punctured by the owner's mean son
If on the road sign Lewis points to some
event   it's miles past Loma where
the orange canyon breaks
and whirlwinds drift on the stone

*

Craggy white peaks   lakes and little
green farms west of here
people in Nashua dream of moving
from the plains   One young teacher from New York
goes west again this year   Someone threw
a bucket of red paint on his old car
Someone else heaped horse dung
on his front porch   Centuries of ice turns
this ground to rock-hard gumbo   I remember the same torn
building in west Texas   Same dry wind   The same
skinny sandpiper weave odd designs around
purple sage   Tonight   wind wants
to tear the roof off this old farmhouse
Up at three   it's lonely as hell the only distant
lights twinkle above the dam

ROOM AT FLATHEAD

Up the creaky stairs a bulb hangs
from a cord in the dark hall
Steam heat rattles marbles through the pipes
And this blue chenille spread wears thin where both
faucets rust the sink   The last roomers
were probably winos trading bed and floor till some farmer's
fence went up   Who could be sadder than women
left in old hotels?   Frayed coat

Pink necklace coiled in a glass
Once a lady and I found a room in San Diego
No windows   Ceiling high as a handball court
and nothing but a cot we hugged on

through the night   Morning
on our way out   juke box
blaring   I glimpsed someone's aunt sleeping
on a barstool   Head on the bar   Red
hair fried to steel wool   Left arm out to anyone
Her face sagged limp
as jelly through the Sunday songs

III.

III.

NIGHT FREIGHT

Under the boarded depot tower
pole lights buzz hot
in the storm and the night diesel thunders
to a stop   Rain drums the tin awning
Pigeon shit streams like paint
Fifty yards down twenty boxcars slam twenty more
and more thunder rumbles the girders
A brakeman walks over   His rubber hood glistens the dark
Ten cars in Bill and I find a door open
to the extra caboose

Hot beans in a can
Little table with seats and electric lamp
We dry out clothes over the stove
Then sit back reading
old newspapers all the way to Reno

After one night in flaming
casinos we hear
stories of freight lurching on her climb
Two heads crushed by a load of pipe
This time on the night freight only this endless wall
of snow   We huddle like sheep in bedrolls
On the steel floor
slow blue flame of the sterno

DEEP IN MOOSE WOODS

Early morning in Glacier
a redwing blackbird zooms through the reeds
and water lilies flame bright goose
feathers in warm sun   Down this path of thick moss
crawdads nudge the bank tender as elephants and raise
explosions of tiny sand clouds
I set my pack under a ponderosa and inside
the willows a she moose lifts her

huge head   Pond mush splashes
from her jowls and her
whole back soaks the color of monk robes
These are woods a lone thief hides in or a mountain

lion chases the doe till she drops
Moose hooves sink stone-heavy
in fresh mud and her haunches shiver the bronze
of horses   Head bowed to the water now
her eyes gleam iodine   Inside the oval onyx
iodine mixed with deep blood
of Mexican saddles

A GROVE OF BLACKBERRIES

September   cold   downtown
Santa Rosa   I lay out
a sheet of plywood under frames of a new
bank   in an hour wake colder
check two churches and walk to the other end of town
Tonight suburban houses are tombs of red brick
Not one window lit up   the first street ends
in a circle   no bushes to crawl into
I try a car   Locked   The next two locked
Tall yellow grass opens white under the moon
Two hours half asleep here and I shudder back into the night
About three some grocer works late inside
a big store and turns away seeing
a living ghost at the window   Someone else left
an old green panel in the lot with a brown
plastic couch in back   I climb over the front seat
and set five cans of oil on the floor
I curl in   Really sleep this time
This time friends and I creak through an old
mansion   The fog rolls in
thick as bushes under the sea

*

Three miles up and away
from the town   I wake to a sheep's
bell clanking below my friends' farm
Two starlings dart past the window to a mustard
yellow birdhouse above the gate

God only knows why I can't wake forever
this way   Sweet smell of rain fields   This lone walk
and hay mounds   the last we'll see stacked round as those
in Brueghel   Ducking into rain-water woods
I find a grove of blackberries my friends must take
for granted   Blackberries bigger
than bumblebees and all the bushes glisten
last night's storm   One loose berry
is a globe of oil beads   A black ruby   It gathers
twenty eyes of blackbirds in an oval bulb and gleams the same
black light I remember once in fever
After furious waves of gold   beads of oil or gems
pulled long moving strings in the dark and each
bright drop shone a purple moon
The grove of blackberries here gathers
so much food any hiker is free to lie down
a whole extra day and
do nothing with the sheep

ST. THERESE OF THE ROSES

In the photo of you standing beside
the white cross   your eyes
shine dark and lucid as a wounded animal's
Friends find you dead and the air smells rose-heavy
as if a big tomb makes space for everyone in your room
Or three gold birds fly up in the total
night   Down and out this spring
I find you again in a beautiful old Spanish
church in Santa Barbara

I lie down on the floor
with memories horrible as the dry grotesque
ghost hooked to a meter in the airport
parking lot of New Delhi

Still there's no real harm sleeping
alone here   The cop for this
quiet neighborhood probably dozes off himself
somewhere out of sight   Both hands folded
on my chest I see your statue lift in the warm shadows
Thirty yellow vigil candles weave and flicker
a thousand ghosts or friends

DINNER AT THE MISSION

Looking back most remember the odd
The retarded girl in yellow
who played for years by a stump full of moss
The fairy tale ragpicker   Or bald giant who pulled
his stumped body through the pool hall
on a tiny cart   In this town
everyone looks away from the guy with forty
rubbery tumors and one ear an inch below the other
Whatever happened to the spooky

sisters who dragged their ghosts
down the street after
an icy fix?   Sweet Jimmy (shoe shine) is gone
And the guy who pawed through trash bins

with a handy salad tweezers
Now it's mainly broken-down winos who
haunt the rich   Look up from
the news before dinner at the mission and three
drag queens float by to strike the world blind
The tall skinny one's afro glows
pink as cotton candy

A MOON FOR THE ROOSTERS

Some things begin exactly for their end
The loner's grocery and gas pump
abandoned by the lake   Three farm boys race out
to have fun and wake sober in the flour dry
cotton of jail smocks   This time begin with the muddied snow
Sixty dollars between two men and a banker's lead-heavy
stare over the plan to ship roosters
Who would dare lend money to drifters probably
sleeping nights in their car   their women and kids left
behind in a filthy trailer in Casper

Old man Jensen in the yard
remembers when four hundred hens to Butte
froze solid as meat in a locker
He leads these guys to a boxcar where crude hutches
go up complete with grain   water and straw

Completely warm with blankets nailed
to the ceiling and walls
A hundred and twenty-eight roosters
perfect friends for a tramp who climbs on and snores
to click of the tracks most the way to Fargo
No wind or blowing snow   Still moonlight
flooding the frosty floor is worth
more than all the gold in the world to a man
and the freezing roosters

OUT OF THE DEPOT TRASH

Quick and tough   Lithe
as whips of willow   They swagger
Jive through   They duck and run
When rats gnaw and scuttle inside the walls
of their house   they hit the streets
Almost every morning now black boys scavenge through
the depot trash and slip in and out of greasy
stalls for pinball and rifle machines
No one but a big cop waiting
for him   this time Bobbie Jordan
steps out in the freezing air and ducks under
the pool hall overhang   Nine years old
and retired from school   he can only raise two bags
of rancid popcorn for breakfast this morning
Out of mountains of junk in sheer
guts of the city   he lifts
a brazed tin pistol from a novelty bin
and it gleams real as the .38 his
uncle once showed him   "This is a holdup"
he tells the bank teller and can't believe his
eyes when she hands over one hundred and eighteen dollars
Back through the depot   down the alley
past Tobey's Place and behind
Big Lil's beauty parlor he races scared
stiff   Then relaxes like a champ
to fork over almost half his loot for a big green
musical watch   This is the first time in his
life he can afford two cheeseburgers at once and a string
of movies that last till midnight

Only nine   the judge lets him off easy
And given the time he needs
he can claim he owns the whole lower
east side if he wants it

ELEPHANT TAMER

August in thick dust of the circus
Two thousand cars roast hot
as stoves   Stained brown tarps smolder
over dozing camels and by noon a little man hoses
down elephants behind the trailers
Docile and dreamy under the icy
flow the big momma sways like a field of mud
Gone the black straw hair   curled tusks
screaming through palms and wiry hunters burning purple
smoke before the hunt   Most people love the small sad eyes
They want elephants to run from the circus or pull
the tent down   Others fight perverse desire
to see the lady trainer crushed
in her act   Here elephants move at the mercy
of a man no bigger than a jockey
He talks to the big one like a child

and brushes swirls of suds on her
legs and back   One light
shove to move her head aside and her tusks show
stubbed and useless horns of a Holstein
The last elephant will die the size of a horse and roam
her final days in white gardens of some neurotic
duchess   The second morning

the little man looks
surprised to see me by the rope again
He takes a peanut from his pocket
and the elephant's trunk drops quick as an insect

Slowly she folds to her knees   rolls over
and her legs curl to four soft posts
Up again   sawdust raining from her back
her obscene nose wriggles a mouth with two holes
Skin brown as a suitcase the little man grins all three
teeth   grabs a bucket and ducks behind
some bales for the hose

EASTER MORNING ON FLATHEAD

Out on the lake this morning
two sails lean away
in the breeze   one white tipped toward
a faster gold one   The same instant a black shepherd
drops a soggy branch on the bank and shakes
a big fuzzball of water
in the air   I remember a perfect
day like this in New York   an old man sat
across the aisle on a subway   Gray derby
Shoes shined like dimes

His bright blue tie matched sky
blue socks   This morning
he could be riding a yacht on the far water
Or sunning himself in a yellow chair

on his porch   Eight wrens
burst like rice
from the restaurant tower and below
three blue-haired ladies jabber the muffled songs
of homing pigeons   Church to breakfast
every event brings them the same surrender now
to lie down   or cold
disappear in the bright grass

IV.

IV

SIX DUCKS IN THE GRAVEL

All night the wind hurled rain
and sleet high as sea
spray over the trees and roofs
It blew the garage door loose and spread
ice over the streets smooth as windows
This morning   sun burns cold in and out of the clouds
It burns cruel where twenty cotton yellow Easter
ducks huddle in a shop display
Most doze in the weak sun till one
waddles toward water and feed in his new home
The man watching from outside keeps his
farm dreams hidden from the world of cars roaring
up Higgins   He turns down an alley off Ryman with a small
white duck carton in his pocket
Two blocks over he heads into the yard
where freight cars slam together
loud as cannons   Where neighborhood boys built
a bonfire on the tracks to meet the train one night
And where sheriff's men pried a drunk loose
who'd froze to the floor of a boxcar
Under quiet of new spring sun
all six ducks wobble out for bread crumbs
in the warm gravel   The man fills a cake
pan for their water trough and leans a stake under
the door of a screened box   Bright ducks in the rocks
Each night huddled in their house
under icy stars   What men building strings
of freight cars would dare question
this old guy's miniature farm?

RIDGE RUNNER

One morning he's spotted three
miles from town and by evening twenty
more up the draw   Quick
as a fox he runs forever to warn deer of fire
or more hunters   One couple claims his scream split
the moon half a mile down from their cabin
Not one word to another human
in years   Then two fires under

the foreman's truck and inside
the cab of a new loader burnt to a crisp
Five men go out the next morning

with rifles   Hair like matted wax
Not four teeth in his whole head
and both eyes stare up shocked wild in the bushes
Knees and elbows stick out hard as a goat's
tied and shivering
in back of Merle's pickup

POEM FOR FAR-OFF CRIES IN THE PORTLAND ZOO

After three weeks rain   today
sun and sky open wide over
the Portland Zoo   All the animals out
black bears sit up for peanuts in cartoon pose
The giant Kodiak spreads out like soup
Even the Bengal tiger paces thirty
feet of cement without a single tree or blade
of grass   Somehow though the day is saved by a hippo
Looking out over the grass and mud
people think there's no one
in this small field   Or maybe
an elephant died   Suddenly they catch
grey flick of the hippo's tail and legs thick as palm
stumps   Obnoxious with dead weight of boulders
her enormous mud-soaked hind
end fills the entrance to her cave

*

Strange how the monkeys'
world changes when they're shipped
to the states   Once riding
stringy vines through palms and sailing through
the air like squirrels   here they climb
and sit inside damp stone buildings
The lonely fluorescent light
inside is the same in swimming pool locker
rooms   And just as wise as anyone
watching the ridiculous orangutan   carrot

red arm and back hair hanging all the way to the floor
chooses to show his rectum to the crowd
Upside down   Head between his
feet   He rolls his eyes like a child
in the straw   Then quick as any dog or fox
he and his little wife scurry to a corner and hide
their sweet affection
under the playground bars

        *

Is it Rebecca's trick on Isaac
brings wrong sacrifice
and abuse of animals through the ages
Or more the drive of Esau
handed down from some unknown Mongolian tribe?
Whatever the reason I thank God for the exaggerated
arrogance of these tough old dusty camels
See how they strut   Or stand forever
in profile   Or simply turn

away from everything that is
not them   No wonder
the giraffe behind the same iron fence
is so mysterious   Even when we feed
her rye crisp from the machine she looks at us
like we are glass   Here the mirror is reversed and
suddenly the animal looks at us from
the other side of the fence
Strange look away wolves   Twenty penguins
in a row are endless people without hands

Not just Portland   We go away from every zoo not having
learned a thing   So the extreme wildness we long
to feel breaks inside the crazed
and terrible cry
of the far-off peacock

SHEEP AND PIGS AT PABLO

In this big orange tin barn
sheep in the far corner
rumble into corrals for the annual
breeders' show   Scrubbed clean   brushed and combed
Tar-black faces point nervous as highbred dogs
I miss the funky sheep on the farm
Once Hank Williams wailed blues on the barn radio
An oval leather halter hung on the wall
Across from the sheep here twenty pigs go berserk on concrete
One blows along the fence

Another blows and snorts
along the floor
A third turns and turns hopeless
for a trough while his mate's hind end keeps
slamming the gate   I remember the hog

fat Rachael's last morning out
she wolfed down a cereal
box like corn   Easy as pie old Ed
leaned over the fence and one clean shot heaved
a rhino on her side   Small pink lids   lead hooves
Rachael's bawl raked the fields
till two quick knives jerked and sputtered
her long human groan

V.

POVERELLO CHRISTMAS

This time no Christmas moon
The only snow freezes
spattered with mud and a light fog drifts
lazy as smoke over the Higgins Bridge
Right at Main there's a guy who hasn't walked these
streets in months   Gray hair matted in a head band
Coat and pants filthy from riding
the freights   Who knows why he walks so fast
carrying a big box filled with cellophane wrappers
I remember bright new chicks brought out of the cold in straw
And small scale of an Irish skiff
with both sails puffed inside the hull

I won't begrudge this old guy
his solitary Christmas with a single fire
by the tracks   God knows there's
plenty to be said for the only birth that stops all the cars
and trains   And releases even a moment
from endless denials

of the poor   The Poverello dinner today
filled with everything
from a blurry-eyed hug to roaring
laughter   One little girl grabbed her doll present
quick with both arms tight   as if I might take
it back   And strange as anyone hauling his empty present
from the street   big Jim Heffernan
held up his new wool socks   eyed them
careful as a plumb bob
making damn sure they fit

MOON OVER THE CHICKEN HUTCH

Out of the east canyon   blowing
snow buries the fence posts
It buries one wall of a barn and this single
truck seems to float past the fuzzball
of a distant farm light   Twenty years ago Arnie Howell
drove into a storm and didn't come back
His uncle Link stood by the grave
Brand new dress shoes soaked in slush
Some nights a Flathead woman wanders this road
toward the dark pine   After ten miles she'll duck inside
the dim orange glow of a bar or behind a trailer door slammed
shut by the wind   She could be.going
nowhere   Or maybe she finds comfort where
these beautiful blue night
lights are spread along the runway

*

I shiver pulling on my clothes
My feet nuzzle a piece
of sheepskin like two white lizards
In a second I'm out the door and back with logs
Fire up in a blast   what to do on a day
like this   I write awhile
Walk down for the paper and mail
Truman Is Dead   In a little story on the next page
some guy named Hartwell survived flying South to the coast
from Yellowknife   After rumbling forever

in terror over the ice the nurse
and pregnant Eskimo died in the wreck
There Hartwell sat one whole month in his silver
plane   Two fractured ankles   A broken knee
And no fire with the boy Kootook
dead the last seven days

*

Under this low orange lamp
my wife sleeps so peaceful nothing's
louder than the clock ticking
on a chair   Outside gusts of snow whirl
against the cabin and the long withdrawing wind sounds
like rain blowing through the pine
The moon is full tonight   Full over snowy hills
I turn out the lamp and see pine trunks rising
in the light   Nights like this drive
a fox insane from her sleep
Not just the moon over snow   Cold wind
riffles her thick fur and her eyes glisten with sight
of the chicken hutch   With timing intricate
as the sky full of stars she moves
swift in a spray of snow
and quiet as the tear of feathers

FOR MEMORY OF A MURDERED WOMAN

In dead of winter no moon
No end to cold where snow buries the pine
woods   Out across the fields a car
rumbles down the road and for no reason deepens
the weight of news   Last night a young woman murdered
in the next town   Amazing how stupid
the chickens when I walk up to the fence
Still gleam of ice in their eyes
shows they feel plenty about terror of death
A knife enters the body with speed of light
A knife enters the heart

and blood from pulsing lake
of the heart's skin glues four ribs together
By morning in the little funeral church a blonde
girl in silk   sleeves puffed blue

as the sky   lifts her flute
and plays about water
There are tears that can't be seen inside
the blood   ''There are tears inside the sparrow's bones''
In 1941 bombs blew the streets away like crusts
of bread   Still Helle Kesma entered
the world held high overhead
her mother wading breast deep through
the sewers of Berlin

THE IRON WALRUS

Empty now where endless wind
cleans it out   this
brick warehouse dies huge as an airplane
hangar   Not one bat in the rafters
Not even footprints of someone ducking out of the snow
Dead still with piled lumber   two steel barrels
and a long rug rolled in the corner
Only soft thunder of a train
a mile down the tracks breaks the silence
Once in a Cleveland museum a huge iron walrus seemed
weightless in the same sunlight

I've always imagined walrus
bighearted buffoons
on the ice   Same watery eyes of seals
Great herds dozing with ears hidden inside their heads
the walrus is duck soup for hunters

Speared   clubbed   shot and driven
north to his last days
the walrus in Cleveland wanted to shed his
thick skin   He saw ivory stacked high
as timber and wanted to float up inside swirling gold
shafts of museum dust   Even in this empty
warehouse only one sparrow
exact color of lead   wants to roost
with a few pigeons

SOUTH END WRECKING

After four long months of snow
and winds from the north
what a relief to work again on soft ground
Early this morning I split some larch
clean to the honey glow of pitch
Fresh as coffee   Fresh as bright shafts of new straw
On the road to town   water runs all along the cliffs
I stop at South End Wrecking and three boys
stand over a mechanic cleaning

lifters in a big can   At first
no one moves   absorbed
in a world ancient as working the first crude
wheels   Or pulling dead weight of a kill

over rolling logs   Gas and oil
smell so old   Old tires
A big rubber hammer   Everything here is dug
from the ground   On the way home purple
willows lace the slough   There's no one else on this
single road   And that old clapboard house on the cliff
See how quiet now on the high
salmon colored stone

TRAMP IN THE DEPOT

Three days and nights on
and off the main line
Drum Gleason tosses up his bedroll
and climbs through the open door of another
boxcar   He brushes away glass and straw
from a corner and sits down
to roll a smoke   A thousand miles
of sage and blowing wheat   with nights on the cold steel
floors   can be hell running anywhere from New York
to this last straight shot into Seattle
In this country   fence   road and track run
perfect lines through the crops
Viewed from an airplane   irrigated
patches of green   The brown farms   And only
dry clumps of elms and willows hold back the wind
Town   depot   one man in the roundhouse
A brakeman drops the switch and ninety boxcars
jerk and bang through the yard
where sparrows lift and
swirl like dust off the tracks

*

Satin sheets   Drapes white
as swan's down with navy
blue chair and sofa   Her little cottage
swept clean as a buddhist temple
And from her windows   view of crisp new sails
leaning away on the lake

After another long six months of work
no wonder the lady doctor escapes
to her retreat under breezy caverns of Canadian pine
In chaos of the jammed depot this morning
a big friendly cop finds her yellow hatbox by the lockers
There must be times the black man in a red mail
hat would love to unload his

luggage cart onto the tracks
Maybe only the tramp
in a big coat sits down at home
with the trains   He peels cellophane from
a small block of cheese and opens wrinkled skin
of an apple with a penknife
When neighborhood boys race across
the fresh buffed floors his deadly scowl sends them out
Home?   A radio announces the Seahawks lost again
and to him the Dow Jones ticker tape might
as well count forty thousand cars
roaring to work   With grace of an old filthy
bear he slices soft little moons from his apple and eats
them off the blade   Exactly nine years ago
after a falling tree crushed four
discs in his spine   he
sat down in his shack and quit

A BREAK FROM THE ROAD

Along this dull flat pull
across the plains   towns like Wasco
and Rufus   Here and there a few
cows and each farm exposed as a boat in the rocks
About noon my wife and I turn into Lewiston
so quiet Sundays these streets could be abandoned on the moon
Under boarded church windows on 21st two boys spray
a dog with blue paint   And farther up
the block three loose sheets have
blown away to the fence   Is the dearth of all
little towns everyone out of school old and the prettiest
women spread wide after the fourth

or fifth child?   We curve up
the town hill where twin
mansions glow swan white in the pine
Then spread our blankets under a rush of lilacs
and lay out the food
Today clouds freeze in streaks

over Lewiston   Thirty swallows
swerve and bank against
nothing in the sky   From here it's clear
the town's money is made from a giant paper mill
on the Clearwater   Any night now three shots in the hills
A knifing   Some disaster will remind everyone
We are still very much alive
and each morning drive
or walk these streets to work

ROAST DOG

In good times   clouds of sparks
rolled from the burners
All five mills thundered two acres of stock-
piled logs and where endless Christmas
bulbs laced suburban hills even a shop foreman drove
a Buick big as a small house
Now the war's shut down the Evans Plant
grinds to a halt   Tonight while the foreman
mulls a new gallows sheet   his harried
wife   up from a migraine nightmare   paces the long floor
without money   Without a single dime and lonely
as any woman   another tramp

on Broadway leans into a news box
Ear flaps open   Big coat
One boot black   One brown   His huge black
face carries all the sorrows of the thirties into
nineteen-eighty   It's fierce wind

howls through Hellgate Canyon
shakes a flimsy lean-to and cakes the tarp
door ice   As times grow worse
any dog in the reeds might
roll and spit nicely over fire for a hungry man
One story claims an early drifter was found by the tracks
Head down   Boots gone   Tied to a tree
His blue hard tongue
was split with a pocket knife

SNOW OF THE HUNDRED FLOWERS

Early morning of the wedding
a priest runs up the church steps
with his arms full of white
mums   He stuffs them into altar baskets
and ties big sky-blue ribbons around slim white
bodies of the wicker   In a brick mansion
on Pine the mother and bride
arrange and rearrange little roses
that hold the wispy veil in place
This is the family who left the grandfather's
farmhouse to swallows roosting in the attic
The barn   ripped down on a weekend   was hauled to town
for rustic siding   Gentle as tending spring lambs
now the priest spreads linen over
the altar white as the wedding gown
He sets down four huge candles in silver
holders with a thud and flicks on
a light that lifts Christ's body with great solemn
wings above the altar stone   Mourning the old
man's death the family served dinner with candles blooming
on his oak table like the last wood
casket on the earth   Everything auctioned

traded and sold   only his ebony
cane remains as if his
whole life was honed down to the smooth
black bone of a walking stick

Harmless once it whacked his great
nanny hog out of the corn rows and gleamed blue
as a gun barrel when he rode his stallion over the lush
meadows   Now the mysterious wand curses
the family where it leans in the basement
of the house on Pine   The old man's
past seeps with apples into the orchard sod
where four generations of farmers
lie buried under sodden hay
This morning everything worth having gleams
new with silk and bright spring snow of the hundred flowers
If ghost of the crochety old grandfather returns
his eyes gleam black as those of Serbian
murderers   His high-buttoned shoes
and wax-smooth pate sour the wedding like some
ancient Hittite priest's   If he brings
flowers for the bride they can only be roses for the furnace
If he brings a prayer in his heart it sings and leaks
under the rocks   It burns and smokes
where a lonely badger
waddles through long river grass

FIRST FREIGHT OUT

August in the noon heat
I wake to drum of boxcars clicking
along the tracks   Outside two
hundred miles of wheat weaves her secret oceans of gold
And right at home a little black man sleeps
sprawled at the other end of the car
Who is he   rising when the train slows?
He lays out a few clothes

that fold into his sack perfect
boxcar   boxcar   boxcar
Careful as ice he slides his bottle of wine in

and ties a quick knot
Alone as the buddha or any monk
he drops to the floor so easy he floats to the ground
PASCO   the sign reads   Here a thousand billion
stars sprinkle out the nights